What Others are Saying About Attitudinal Healing

"After 25 years and more than 30,000 guests, it was Jerry Jampolsky's definition of forgiveness that changed my life."
— *Oprah Winfrey*

"Attitudinal Healing is a way of looking at life and death and pain squarely in the eye and even overcoming it."
— *Morely Safer, 60 Minutes*

"Attitudinal Healing has changed my life. It has helped me let go of the obstacles to love and I can recommend it with all of my heart."
— *Carlos Santana*

"Attitudinal Healing has supported many of the Sisters living in community and working with the poor."
— *Mother Teresa*

AGING WITH ATTITUDE

Aging WITH Attitude

Gerald G. Jampolsky, M.D.
Diane V. Cirincione, Ph.D.

MINI COURSE PUBLISHING
Sausalito, California

Cover design: Mariah Parker
www.mettagraphics.com

MINI COURSE PUBLISHING
www.minicourseforlife.com
3001 Bridgeway, Suite K-368
Sausalito, CA 94965
877-244-3392

We lovingly dedicate this book to Jack Luckett and Eulalia Luckett, the two people who have deeply inspired us to live a life filled with unconditional love and forgiveness.

They have influenced so many around the world with their attitudes about life, love, joy and laughter regardless of their circumstances or the challenges they have encountered.

ACKNOWLEDGMENTS

It is with deepest appreciation that we thank Hal Zina Bennett, our long time editor, and our graphic designer, Mariah Parker, for their unmeasurable talent, unlimited patience, and most importantly, true friendship.

We would also like to acknowledge Helen Schucman, Bill Thetford, Judith Skutch Whitson and Bill Whitson, who have each played such important roles in our lives, helping us to experience another way of looking at the world through the gift of *A Course in Miracles*.

CONTENTS

INTRODUCTION

As we find ourselves growing older, many of us may also find ourselves as caregivers for our aging parents. Or perhaps we have a close friend who is now requiring the help of a caregiver. It is not unusual for these situations to set off fears associated with our own aging.

There are those of us who have seen a parent or loved one suffering from the symptoms of Alzheimer's disease, or other forms of dementia. We may find ourselves fearing that the same could happen to us.

There are so many issues associated with aging, everything from memory loss to falling and having an injury that causes us to be more dependent on others.

Perhaps you've noticed that your empathy for a friend's suffering has aroused your fears about almost everything that might affect your own life.

And given the economic instability we've witnessed in recent years, perhaps you fear that you won't have enough money to live independently and possibly lose your ability to make choices about how you live.

Any one of us might put together a list of fears that we are imagining. It has been our experience that the biggest fear most of us have, either consciously or unconsciously, is the fear of dying.

And on top of everything else, we're all bombarded by the media about how important it is to look and act as if we were years younger than our biological age, as if the reality of our age was something of which we should be ashamed.

The purpose of this book is to share with you that there is another way of looking at the world and another way of looking at the aging process.

You do not have to fear that you are a victim of your aging. All of our negative, fearful attitudes can be changed by healing our attitudes.

In the pages ahead we'll explore how each of us has an opportunity to live the later years of our lives with inner peace, happiness, and tranquility, regardless what may be happening to our bodies and our minds.

We'll discover that all our fears about aging are reversible, and that love is more powerful than fear.

This book focuses on unconditionally forgiving others and ourselves as the key

to happiness and inner peace, and that we
experience love when we actually let
go of fear.

Chapter 1

ATTITUDE IS EVERYTHING

We know that our happiness, and how well we feel we have lived our lives, is not determined by the level of our education or by how much money we have or by how many things we have amassed. It is not determined by the job titles or positions we have held. Neither is it determined by the number of friends we have made or by the experiences we have had in the past.

Happiness and feeling good about the lives

we are now living are most profoundly determined by the attitudes we hold in our minds. In actuality, how we experience everything in our lives is ultimately determined by our attitudes. Therefore, healing our attitudes becomes a major stepping stone toward enjoying a happy and fulfilling life.

Attitudinal Healing is based on the premise that ultimately it is not other people, events, or experiences in the past that are causing us to be upset or stressed out. Rather, it is our thoughts, attitudes, and judgments about those things that cause our distress. We may not be able to change others. And we know we cannot change the past. But we can change our perceptions of these in the present.

As we get older we may be prone to worrying more. Or maybe we become more impatient, complaining, and short tempered. We may find that happiness is more difficult to experience.

And we may start to feel that our physical and mental capabilities are slowly diminishing.

Is it just possible that our culture is putting too much emphasis on our bodies and not enough focus on the thoughts and attitudes that we put into our minds?

Is it possible that there is another way of looking at the world and our beliefs about our bodies, minds, and spirits?

Is it possible that our true reality is spiritual and not physical?

And is it possible that we have unintentionally created a fearful ego mind that makes us afraid that when we die it is the end of life?

What would happen to our fears of so many things, including aging, if we started to believe that perfect love has the power to cast out all fear?

Is it possible that our attitudes play a pivotal

role in determining how we deal with life, health and aging? And is it possible that our attitudes help to determine whether our relationships are loving and peaceful or full of conflict and fear?

The Most Important Gift We Are Given

Perhaps the most important gift that the universe has given us is the freedom to choose what thoughts and attitudes we put in our minds. Are you willing to imagine what would happen to you, and to the life you live, if you truly thought it was of value to believe that love can heal any problem you now have, or any problem that you will have in the future?

By changing our belief system, by letting love become more important than fear, we can grow older with grace and be happy and peaceful inside—regardless of what is happening on the outside or the condition of our bodies.

The Essence of Our Being

In our work in Attitudinal Healing over the last four decades, we utilize twelve principles of practical spirituality. The first principle is: The Essence Of Our Being Is Love.

To us this means that our true reality is more than these temporary bodies in which we live. We are Unconditional Love, a formless, never-ending Energy of Light that is part of All That Is and can never be extinguished.

We have chosen to believe that by changing our belief system and having faith and trust in a Higher Power, Love becomes the answer to all our problems, and to all the Fears of Aging or any other fears we may be hanging onto. As we choose to change our belief system, Love, our Spiritual Core, becomes our only reality.

When we experience a moment of healing through the higher consciousness of forgiving the world, our past, ourselves and all others, and by giving our unconditional Love to help another, all judgments, grievances and fears can begin to fade away.

When we are in this healing moment we are not focusing on the past or future. We are living only in that present instant of unconditional love and peace, where there is no fear about anything.

It is our fear, judgments, and guilt that block us from experiencing Love as our true and natural state of being. The gift of loving another person without any judgments is one of the greatest gifts we can give to another or ourselves.

♥

A few years ago an 82-year-old woman came in to see Jerry. She had moved to a nearby retirement community from Southern California specifically because she wanted to start an Aging with Attitude Support Group at her new home and wanted him to help her.

Within a short time, the group was started with seniors from ages 65 to 94. Many of the members felt anxious and depressed about the future while others had both physical and cognitive challenges.

As the group continued throughout the years, many of these symptoms reportedly lessened.

It was our impression that because the members of the group were feeling both helpful and useful to others, that they received as much as they gave, and the attitudinal healing was palpable.

Through forgiveness, many who formerly were complainers stopped complaining. They frequently forgave their adult children and other family members who were not in contact with them as much as they would have liked. Overall, they were happier and were messengers of love and forgiveness wherever they went.

About that time there was a popular national television program called The Hugh Downs Show. It was about people in advanced years finding happiness. Our people went on the show with Jerry. They shared their experiences that by changing their attitudes they succeeded in changing their lives. They taught others around the country that we can be happy and peaceful regardless of our age, circumstances, what is happening to our bodies, or what limitations we may have in our lives.

They also pointed out how important forgiveness is for removing the blocks to love and peace, and how quickly love replaces fear when we forgive others or ourselves.

They demonstrated that when each morning they committed to have a happy day, no matter what happened in that day, they usually ended up having a happy day.

Learning to create healthier attitudes is a way of having more peace and harmony each day.

We have found the following guidelines can be extremely helpful in changing our attitudes about the way we look at the world.

Rather than focusing on our own fears around aging, it can be helpful to ask ourselves, throughout the day, "In what ways can I be more loving and helpful to others? How can I be a better listener? How can I be more accepting, more compassionate and less judgmental?"

Healing our attitudes is the process of:

- Seeing the value of consciously choosing peace instead of conflict in every situation
- Choosing love instead of fear
- Choosing patience instead of impulsivity
- Choosing to be gentle to others and ourselves

- Choosing to be a love-finder instead of fault-finder
- Choosing to be a love-giver rather than a love-seeker
- Choosing to count our smiling wrinkles instead of our aging wrinkles
- Deciding each day to teach and demonstrate unconditional love.

(For more information on Attitudinal Healing, including *A Mini Course for Life*, go to www.ahinternational.org.)

Chapter 2

Forgiveness is the Key to Happiness

As we age there is more fear about the possible declining abilities of our bodies and the diminished capacity of our minds. Along with this, we can be preoccupied with fears about facing our own dying.

Maybe we worry more about how many years we have left or whether we are going to have pain or be alone when we pass. Sometimes we can have a tendency to blame the world and to feel that the world is unfair. Perhaps we want our loved ones nearby in our last days but fear they might not be there. All these fears can mount up to judgments that can cause us to feel unwanted, unappreciated, and unloved.

Worrying and being fearful does not help us resolve these fears nor does it bring us more peace. On the contrary our fearfulness makes us distressed and unhappy.

Getting older does not have to be associated with fear, unhappiness, or the loss of inner peace. We can turn things around when we develop an attitude of forgiveness rather than fear.

The most important gift that we have is the ability to choose what thoughts we have in our minds and what attitudes we hold about others.

Forgiveness can play an important part in bringing about a new way of experiencing our lives.

Forgiveness—The Greatest Healer of All

To forgive is the prescription
for happiness;
To not forgive is the prescription
to suffer.

Is it possible
all pain
regardless of its cause
has some component of
unforgiveness in it?

To hold on to vengeful thoughts
to withhold our love and compassion
certainly must interfere
with our health
and our immune system.

Holding on to what we call
justified anger
interferes with our experiencing
inner peace.

To forgive
does not mean
agreeing with the act;
it does not mean condoning
an outrageous behavior.

Forgiveness means
no longer living in
the fearful past.

Forgiveness means
no longer scratching the wounds
so they continue to bleed.

Forgiveness means
living and loving
completely in the present,
without the shadows of the past
or the fear of the future.

Forgiveness means
freedom from anger
and attack thoughts.

Forgiveness means
letting go of all hopes
for a better past.

Forgiveness means
not excluding
your love from anyone.

Forgiveness means
healing the hole in your heart
caused by unforgiving thoughts.

Forgiveness means
seeing the light
in everyone, regardless
of their behavior.

Forgiveness is not just for
the other person – but for ourselves
and the mistakes we have made,
and the guilt and shame we still hold on to.

Forgiveness in the deepest sense
is forgiving ourselves
for separating ourselves from one another.

To forgive this very instant
means no longer being
King or Queen of the Procrastinator's Club.

It is never too early
to forgive.
It is never too late
to forgive.

How long does it take
to forgive?
It depends on your belief system.

If you believe it will never happen,
It will never happen.

If you believe it will take six months,
It will take six months.

If you believe it will take but a second,
That's all that it will take.

We believe with all our hearts
That peace will come to the world
When each of us takes the
Responsibility of forgiving everyone,
Including ourselves, completely.

Why We Do Not Want to Forgive

When we choose not to forgive it is usually because our fearful ego minds tempt us to believe that if we forgive someone it is an act of weakness. Not forgiving is a waste of time because it does not control the other person or prevent them from doing the same unforgivable things again. But if you forgive someone, you will feel more secure. These are common reasons we buy into as to why we do not forgive:

The ego mind does not want us to feel at peace and wants to entrap us into believing that there is only a past and future rather than seeing the benefit of living in the present. The ego wants us to live in the hurtful past and to predict that the future will be just the same. The ego's enemy is inner peace; it believes that you can find security when you hurt another back after you have been hurt by them.

In previous decades forgiveness was never mentioned in a physician's training. Times have changed. We have given lectures and held seminars in numerous medical schools on the role of forgiveness in medicine and, today, it is much more commonplace.

When I, Jerry, became legally blind in both eyes, there was a temptation coming from my fearful ego to find someone or something to blame. It was tempting to blame my body or my genes and to have anger towards my body.

One of the key principles of Attitudinal Healing is that forgiveness is the key to happiness. Remembering this, I changed my mind and chose to no longer make my body and my eyes my enemy. I forgave my body for not being what I had wanted it to be.

We find that frequently people at our stage in life are still holding onto unforgiving thoughts about themselves or others. This often can interfere with the effectiveness of the medication or healing modality. It is amazing that when we become aware, even when we are in the process of dying, how important it is not to be holding onto grievances of any kind.

Preparation for retraining our minds begins with seeing the value of learning to quiet our minds, so that we are not caught up in the busyness of the day. If you meditate, you might start there.

Meditation simply means having a peaceful mind—which is our natural state—one that is tranquil and still. Clarity then becomes possible because there are no conflicting thoughts, judgments, or fears.

Have a willingness to be open-minded as you review the following principles. Remind yourself that it is all right to disagree with or reject any of these thoughts. Forgiveness is a choice, and you do not have to forgive or believe in forgiveness. But do your best to look at the consequences of your choice to forgive or not forgive, letting your heart help you decide.

One key word, willingness, gives you the power to move ahead in the forgiveness process. This occurs when you go into action and say to yourself, with full trust, that there is great value in letting go of all of your grievances and anger toward others and yourself.

- Decide that you are no longer going to suffer from the boomerang effect of your unforgiving thoughts.

- Remember that in forgiving, you are not agreeing with the other person or condoning their hurtful behavior.

- You may find it helpful to write a letter to the person you wish to forgive. Express all of your feelings, and then tear up the letter.

- Believe that holding on to anger does not bring you what you really want.

- Believe that holding onto grievances and unforgiving thoughts is a way for you to suffer.

- Believe that everyone you meet is a teacher of patience.

- Recognize the value of giving up all your judgments.

- Believe that you have the power to choose the thoughts you put in your mind.

- Be clear that your only goal is peace of mind, not changing or punishing another person.

- Be willing to count your blessings rather than your hurts.

- Rather than seeing people as attacking you, see them as fearful and giving you a call of help for love.

- Recognize that any emotional pain you feel at any moment is caused by your own thoughts about someone or something.

- Be willing to see this person who hurt you as one of your greatest teachers, giving you the opportunity to really learn what forgiveness is all about.

- Remember that in the process of forgiving the other person, you are forgiving yourself.
- Enjoy the happiness and peace that comes from forgiving.

As we get older many of us find that we are separated from our families and holding on to grievances because perhaps our adult children are not visiting us enough. Whenever we are unhappy about external situations or when something goes wrong, we often find someone else to blame.

We have helped people create the first Attitudinal Healing peer support groups for senior citizens where they feel valued and useful in helping each other. They no longer see value in complaining or to holding onto judgments because they give and receive unconditional love within the group. When we feel loved and are giving that love away, we find that we are far happier and at peace with life.

Oftentimes, older adults complain that: "As I was getting older I believed I would be experiencing the Golden Years of my life. Instead, I am feeling more challenges around my lessening independence and what appears to be the deterioration of my abilities and my body."

There was a woman in her 80's who was waiting to be shown her room in her new senior living situation. The administrator who was accompanying her explained that it was their policy to get each person's approval. The woman smiled as he explained this. When he was done, she said, "Oh, that won't be necessary." Perplexed, the administrator said he wanted her to see the room to determine whether or not she liked it. She said, "Oh, I am sure I will. You see, I already made up my mind that I would like it before I came here."

We are never too old to heal our attitudes and change our minds about how we look at aging.

Chapter 3

CHANGE YOUR MIND ABOUT AGING AND CHANGE YOUR LIFE

Worrying and being fearful does not bring us resolution to any fears we have around aging, nor does it bring us more peace. On the contrary worry and fear can make us feel distressed and unhappy. But it doesn't have to be this way.

The most important gift that we have is the ability to choose the thoughts we have in our minds and what attitudes we hold about others. We can turn things around when we develop an attitude of forgiveness rather than fear.

♥ PHYLLIS GIRARD

My (Diane's) mother, Phyllis, lived near us at the wonderful Redwoods Retirement Community in Mill Valley, California until her passing at 94 years of age. She was a beloved and remarkable woman who lived her life to the fullest by overcoming seemingly insurmountable odds. Where there was no love, she put love, and then found love. Obstacles became challenges from which she never shied away.

As the 14th of 16 children of Italian-American immigrant parents, Phyllis developed resilience and determined thinking on her own. She used these qualities to survive both physically and emotionally in very challenging times. When she was young she had next to no say about her choices in life. She was denied an education beyond 8th grade even though she begged to go to High School like her other siblings. She was punished for playing the piano in her determined pursuit to learn. She was denied friends and non-work related social interaction. And she longed to emulate her heroine, the aviator Amelia Earhart.

Over the course of her life, Phyllis broke down barriers for herself, and thus influenced her children to do the same. She often said to me, "Don't let anyone ever limit your world."

At age 75 and in the presence of all her children, grandchildren and great grandchildren, she became the oldest woman to graduate from her college (with high honors I might add) and the first and only of her siblings to ever do so. She learned to play the piano and the organ and even tried out the guitar. She was beloved beyond description by friends and members of her church and her community. In mid-life she overcame a fear of flying by learning how to fly a single engine plane and solo. She overcame her fear of the water by getting her 100 feet scuba diving certificate in her late fifties.

Phyllis chose to have an attitude of gratitude, regardless of her circumstances, and she was determined to make good choices for herself as she increased in age. Having a restricted childhood with so few choices, she valued her power to choose the thoughts she put in her mind, especially later in life.

Rather than complaining and holding onto grievances, Phyllis focused on being kind to everyone who worked where she lived, regardless of their position. She was grateful for life, her faith, and everyone and everything around her.

In her last years, it was important for my siblings and me to know how she was doing and what was going on when we were not there, so that we could be advocates for her if and when necessary. When we asked her how she was doing, she always said, "Now remember; I am not complaining. I am just explaining!"

One of her favorite statements each day was, your attitude is everything! One can be happy and peaceful on the inside regardless of what is happening to their body and regardless of their circumstances.

In her final years, Phyllis began to have moderate and then more serious memory loss. Rather than being upset about these losses, as many of us are sometimes, Phyllis came up with this statement that impressed us tremendously. She said: "You know, not being able to remember is not all that bad. You see, I can no longer remember what I was upset about."

Phyllis was nearly always in a state of gratitude. She was always thanking the staff and everyone else including her family for all they do for her—even with the most seemingly insignificant deeds. We rarely saw her without a smile even though her body was being ravaged with numerous internal maladies. One of her badges of honor is that she became so well after a year in Hospice care that she was graduated out!

Death was never an enemy to Phyllis nor was she ever afraid of it. She had a few near death experiences and knew that a continuation of life awaited her beyond the life of the body. While it was hard for her to leave us all here, she was ready to depart this life when the time finally came.

One of the greatest gifts Phyllis gave us, next to her capacity to love unconditionally, was her comfort with death and dying. When times were tough, she often quoted the book *Growing Old Is Not for Sissies.* While aging was challenging for her body and her mind, Phyllis left us a legacy that has changed those that knew her in deep and profound ways. She was an amazing teacher of love, teaching us that it is possible to be happy and full of gratitude, and to be fearless with your last breath.

♥ LARRY GIRARD

Larry Girard was Diane's stepfather. He had a 40 year career at Trans World Airline, including being airport Chief Pilot in the New York area. He was a wonderful guy who played golf and tennis regularly and was quite involved in life. He was also a great storyteller, with accents and all.

Early in the 1980's education about the realities of transmission of AIDS was still unconfirmed and most citizens were terrified of it, or of anyone who had it, fearing that it might be contagious. Larry was no exception.

Early one Christmas morning Jerry was

getting ready to go to San Francisco to visit AIDS patients who were living their last days at a half-way house. He had a number of roses with him which he was planning to quietly place by each person's bedside prior to their awakening.

Jerry was surprised when Larry suddenly asked if he could go with him. Jerry, of course, welcomed him but was honestly surprised as he was acutely aware of Larry's fear of AIDS. They wound up being at the halfway house for over three hours, and Larry spent most of the time observing and being friendly. The shift in Larry's energy was palpable.

Three months later Larry decided, with the help of his wife Phyllis, to start a halfway house where AIDs patients would be able to live free of charge in the Monterey area. Larry and Phyllis would also have people with AIDS come to their house as their guests, where they would have dinner and stay overnight.

Larry chose to change his fearful attitude about persons with AIDS which literally resulted in changing his life in a most positive way.

During Larry's last three years of life he became ill with Lewy Body Disease, one of the most common causes of disability and dementia in the elderly, with a general decline in physical as well as cognitive abilities. This was a very challenging time and much to our surprise, Larry decided to go to an Attitudinal Healing Support Group for persons with chronic and life threatening illnesses. While we never knew the confidential content of any of his many group meetings, it was obvious that Larry was receiving so much from his efforts to attend.

We remember Larry saying that although he was a very private person, he found the Attitudinal Healing Group to be an amazingly safe place because everyone listened with open hearts and were full of love. Perhaps most important, no one was making any judgments of anyone else—they were listening with love.

One day Larry came home after an Attitudinal Healing Group and shared what he had experienced there.

"Today I had an amazing experience," he told us. "For the first time in my life, I took off my last mask and I cried and cried and cried…in front of all the other people there. They just held me as I wept. It was a beautiful experience for me to feel that freedom and trust. I think I am learning to be transparent and to not be afraid of what people might think of me if they know what is going on inside me."

Both Phyllis and Larry demonstrated how we can let go of fear when we let go of judgments and the fear of judgments. Larry demonstrated that we are never too old to release ourselves, our fears, and our vulnerability, and that happiness and freedom can come to us regardless of our age. He passed on with much peace when he was 83 years of age.

♥ DIANA NYAD

Diana never gave up on her goal and her dream of swimming the 103 miles of Florida Straits, from Cuba to Key West without a shark cage. It took her five tries and 35 years, but she finally succeeded at age 64.

She tried to make the swim the first time in 1978 but wasn't successful, so she moved on with her life and pursued other interests. Then, after turning 60 and the passing of her mother, the dream sparked and came alive again.

After her swim she stated, "You are never too old to make your dream come true."

Diana is a wonderful teacher for all of us,

teaching us that we have choices about how we see the challenges before us each and every day.

"All of us suffer heartaches and difficulties in our lives," she said. "If you say to yourself, find a way, you'll make it through."

We can choose to let go of our fears and perceived limitations. We can let go of our negative imaginings and start practicing positive imagination in our lives. Diana imagined that she could succeed—and she did. She didn't do it perfectly, and she made mistakes along the journey. She used her mind to determine the outcome of what she dreamed. And although she failed often, in the end, when age and odds were radically against her, she succeeded not only at achieving her dream but at being her very best self.

May we remember that there is power in the ability of our thoughts to create our reality whether we realize it or not. Negative thoughts create a negative reality just as positive thoughts help create a positive one. Let us continue to see value in our positive thoughts about how we relate to ourselves, each other, and to the challenges in our lives. Let us remember that it is only our own thoughts and attitudes that hurt us. It is only our own self-forgiveness and love that sets us free.

♥ ARNIE BEISSER

Arnie Beisser was Jerry's roommate when he started medical school at Stanford University School of Medicine in 1946. At that time, the medical school was located in San Francisco. Jerry and Arnie became inseparable in spirit. Arnie was a great tennis player and was ranked 9th in the U.S. at the time.

As he was about to start his internship, shockingly, Arnie came down with polio. His paralysis was so extensive that he was in an iron lung. No one knew if he was going to make it. When he finally pulled through, he was quadriplegic.

Arnie did not believe in limitations. He believed that your mind knows no limitations.

He decided to become a psychiatrist and later had a private practice. He also became a professor at UCLA Medical School and later married Rita, his Occupational Therapist.

He was very clever at not getting caught up in the fears and limitations that others might try to put on him. For example, one time when Jerry was visiting him, he shared the following story. He said a casual friend asked how tough it was to live his life in a wheelchair. Arnie's reply was, "I do not choose to go where that question would take me. But what about asking me to tell you about all the things I can do in a wheelchair?"

He refused to dwell on negative thoughts or things.

During his life I (Jerry) talked to him almost every day for forty-five years. I took him with me in my heart and mind and would talk to him from China or Russia or wherever I was lecturing. We shared the inner linings of our hearts together.

Arnie taught me what a true friendship is all about. For us it was someone who does not judge you and loves you unconditionally, no matter what you do or have done.

Arnie demonstrated every moment of his of life that your attitude is everything.

♥ MOTHER TERESA

It was our honor, pleasure, and joy to know and work with Mother Teresa and the Missionaries of Charity for several years.

Much of Mother Teresa's great work was with the dying, the poor, and the elderly. Her commitment to being a messenger of unconditional love and peace spread globally.

She inspired priests, nuns and lay persons all over the world. She believed nothing was impossible. She was fearless.

Whether she was with people who were dying, or where she demonstrated kindness and compassion to those who were living on the streets, or when she was with the aged or poor, she demonstrated unconditional love with a total absence of judgments. And through her love Mother Teresa gave dignity and hope to all. And by her example, she taught others to do the same.

Mother Teresa once said that one of the biggest problems in the world is that people are suffering from "Spiritual Deprivation," and that love was the solution to every problem we face. Her message of love traveled across borders, cultures, and faiths.

Mother Teresa believed that love was the most powerful healing agent in the world.

She believed that regardless of what the fear was about, whether it was about dying, aging, or lack of money, surrendering to Love and respecting the dignity of others would bring everyone to a consciousness of love, peace and happiness.

Mother Theresa was particularly helpful to the aged and to those who were facing imminent death. She and her Sisters gave the comfort of unconditional love to so many who would have otherwise died alone, helping them experience the power of love in relinquishing fear as they faced death.

Mother Theresa demonstrated the power of how just one person can make such an extraordinary difference in this world.

There is no way of sharing the great effect that she and the Missionaries of Charity, and those with whom they worked, inspired us and helped to change our lives.

♥ JACK AND EULALIA LUCKETT

Most everyone has someone they emulate and look up to. We are no exceptions. When it comes to dealing with the mental, emotional, and physical challenges often connected to aging, Jack and Eulalia Luckett are our heroes!

For over forty years the Lucketts have not only been our dearest of friends, but exemplary pioneers in their attitudes about aging and life in general.

Jack, a retired Marine Colonel, hero of the Korean War, and former Assistant District Attorney in Los Angeles, was an early Executive Director of the first Center for Attitudinal Healing in Tiburon, California.

Eulalia was one of the first women to graduate from the Harvard MBA program. They have been married over 45 years.

Eulalia is 77 years young and Jack is 87. They are, without exception, two of the happiest people we know—not just today but throughout the decades that we have known them, through weighty tragedies and everyday life.

Both of their lives have been directed towards achievement and worldly success. In anyone's eyes, they had it all. They had brains, beauty, style, status, money, and success in all they had attempted and in their related fields. What more could they want or need? How about inner peace, joy, and lasting happiness? It is our impression that this is what they lacked.

In the mid-1970's they both sought and found a spiritual path that inspired them to change their lives. From lives of doing, achieving, and succeeding, they committed themselves to living their lives without judging others and to giving and receiving unconditional love. They no longer pursued physical possessions; instead, they downsized their living situation to live as simply and peacefully as they could. To many, this would seem like a supreme sacrifice, but to them it represented freedom and opened them to joy.

The Luckett's both know that their happiness is definitely a matter of choice and that their peace of mind comes from a connection with a Higher Source with harmony and integrity in all that they think, say, and do. They know what they are…part of All That Is.

All of us have an innocent child inside, and Jack and Eulalia allow theirs to come out and play—something so many adults are afraid or embarrassed to do. They laugh often and can act in silly ways without being fearful of censure, disapproval, or judgment because they know who they are. And because of their uninhibited joy and exuberance, people are drawn to them and are nourished in their presence.

Do not mistake simple for easy. They are not exempt from the challenges that we all face. We have seen them deal with aging, illness, death, and relationship problems as well as the mundane difficulties of everyday life just like the rest of us.

The difference is that they have accepted the fact that they have the ability to choose peace over conflict, and love over fear, in any given circumstance on any given day. The knowledge that they have the ability to choose the attitudes they have about anything, anyone, or any set of circumstances, gives them the unlimited power to decide how they are going to experience life and each other.

That, and precisely that—the ability to make all their choices motivated by love instead of fear— generates a life of joy and happiness during the journey of aging, regardless of what the world presents to them.

♥ JOAN WALSH ANGLUND

Forty years ago, I, Jerry, received a Valentine's card from a person I did not know. Later in the day, I reread the card and noticed it was actually an original drawing, not one you buy in the stationery store. The name on the card was Joan Walsh Anglund. I decided to call Joan and we had an amazing, long conversation.

Joan had sent the Valentine's card to me after seeing a TV special produced by Phil Donahue. The program was the first of its kind featuring children who were facing life-threatening diseases and were discovering new ways to handle the challenges associated with their diagnosis. I had been working with these children at the original Center for Attitudinal Healing located in Tiburon, California.

Immediately, Joan and I became soul mates and have continued our deep spiritual relationship since that first telephone conversation. Diane met Joan soon after we met and quickly fell in love with Joan, too.

Joan has published 141 books to date that have sold over 50 million copies around the world, in 17 languages. Two of her most famous illustrated books are *A Friend is Someone Who Likes You* and *Love is a Special Way of Feeling*. For more than 50 years, in addition to writing and illustrating books, she has produced greeting cards, dolls, figurines, glassware and a host of other creative products. Many celebrities have been counted as Joan's devoted fans including, Eleanor Roosevelt, Queen Elizabeth, Cary Grant, Jackie Kennedy Onassis, Carol Burnett, Julie Andrews, Elizabeth Taylor, and the Emperor of Japan.

Although many of her books are written for children, they are equally enjoyable and meaningful to adults. Diane and I are honored that Joan dedicated one of her books to the Center for Attitudinal Healing in Tiburon, California.

In January of this year, Joan celebrated her 90th birthday. When asked "How old do you really feel inside?" she replied, "Oh, about 40! It's amazing how much creative energy I still have." Since her 90th birthday, she has already written two new books that are scheduled to be published soon.

Joan has had amazingly close relationships with her two children, Thaddeus and Joy, her granddaughter Emily, and her 5-year-old twin great-granddaughters, Peach and Rose. Much of her life now centers on nourishing her great grandchildren and enjoying the love of her family.

Neither Diane nor I have ever experienced Joan having a negative judgment toward anyone. Her heart is full of goodness. Her enthusiasm for life and her caring about others is beyond measure. Whether she is with an old friend or a new acquaintance, the loving energy that comes from her heart makes that person feel that this is the most important moment of Joan's life.

It has not always been an easy, unchallenging life for Joan. Her son died at an early age and later, her husband Bob died. When tragedy happens, some people hold onto the pain forever and often times hold on to anger about their painful past. In our experience, Joan just doesn't get stuck in the painful past. She lives totally in the present, seeing herself as a messenger of love. She knows that is why she is here. She is totally unafraid of dying and believes that her true reality is Spirit, not just a body.

Not only is Joan not caught in loss or anger but she is committed to seeing the light of love in everyone, regardless of their behavior. She is truly a light in an oftentimes darkened world. People tend to see that in her, and through her reflection they can see the light in themselves.

Looking past everyone's behavior makes Joan a love finder instead of a fault finder. Rather than judging people, she celebrates each person as a unique expression of individuality. There is a sparkle in her eyes that brings everyone who knows her into the center of her love and into the Love that created us all.

In January a friend mentioned Joan's 90th birthday on Facebook. Joan was overwhelmed by the response to that Facebook post when more than 2,500 people sent her birthday greetings.

Joan loves life. She demonstrates in an almost timeless way that Love is our only reality. It's easy to see that she is not afraid of getting older. She doesn't think of her age in terms of numbers. She keeps the innocent child alive in her heart and mind.

Joan is totally committed to her spiritual pathway and to celebrating kindness, patience and compassion in all of her interactions. It is a blessing for us to be such close and intimate friends with her and to have a relationship where the three of us continue to love and grow in our attitudes around aging.

Joan does not believe that anything is impossible...and neither do we.

Chapter 4

SPIRITUAL VISION

As we begin our seventh and ninth decades of life, we do our best to shine our Light and to see the Light in others regardless of their behavior. We do our best to remember that love is letting go of form and our attachment to a script for our lives. We remind ourselves often that we are not victims of the world we see, but co-creators and producers of our own experiences.

Part of having spiritual vision is seeing past our own as well as others' illusions—choosing to see the Light in others and knowing it is but a reflection of the Light in us. We love using our friend Fred Matser's wonderful motto, "Let us go through life with miles and miles of smiles," to inspire each other and to feel better about ourselves and our lives.

Spiritual vision is choosing to look through the eyes of love and not fear as we go through life. We know that our unresolved, negative thoughts create negative experiences fueled by our fears, and that what we perceive in the world is a direct reflection of the thoughts in our minds.

Spiritual vision is experiencing the world through love's eyes and not through our body's ego eyes of fear.

More and more we are remembering that the only thing that is real, and that never changes, is our united connection with our Source.

We believe that our spiritual vision has a DNA

of happiness, unconditional love, kindness, tenderness, and gentleness, celebrating light and love, and seeing only love wherever we go, for that is what we are. It is celebrating freedom from our self-imposed ego prisons.

For me, Jerry, utilizing spiritual vision is remembering that I am blind when I judge others and interpret their behavior based on what I see only through my physical eyes. And I am sighted when I remind myself that I am not my past or my glaucoma, nor is my identity limited to my body. The essence of my being is love. My spiritual vision is seeing everyone and everything through the filter of love in my heart and in my mind.

I have been blessed by having Diane as my spiritual partner who is completely committed to choosing her spiritual path. Diane has been an amazing teacher of unconditional love, gentleness, kindness and compassion, not only for me but for so many others.

There are some times when I forget completely that I have a choice in how I see the world. At those times everything I see appears so real and so deserving of my judgments. Mother Teresa once told Diane and me that, "No one is always following a loving, spiritual path but it is our intentionality of going in that direction that counts." At this moment I am determined to see everything through kind, loving and non-judgmental eyes.

I am legally blind but my spiritual vision is getting better all the time!

Diane and I like to be playful at the gym where we work out so that the exercises we do will be less boring. So on occasion I will come up behind Diane when she is on a stationary bike and kiss her on the cheek. And there are times that she will do the same with me.

Well, one day I came up behind Diane to give

her a kiss on the cheek and all of a sudden I realized that I was kissing another woman! But there is some humor here at the gym. I have been nick-named the Blind Kisser!

We know how blessed we are. We try to go through life with the goal of dissolving any thoughts of loss or separation in our lives by enhancing love, forgiveness, compassion, kindness and humor.

Chapter 5

AGING WITH ATTITUDE GUIDELINES

The people we know who go through the aging process with the greatest happiness and peace of mind, seem to be following at least some of the guidelines we list below. As you read through the list you'll probably discover that you are already familiar with many of these guidelines. We suggest taking one or two guidelines a day and imagining them becoming a part of your heart. You might want to write down on a card the guideline you're working on at any given time and taking that card with you as a reminder throughout the day.

1. Choose to no longer see value in holding on to guilt.

2. Resist the temptation to interpret people's behavior to decide who is "innocent" and who is "guilty."

3. Choose to make forgiving others and yourself as important as breathing.

4. Choose to not take yourself too seriously.

5. Choose to keep a good sense of humor about yourself.

6. Begin to see no value in anger or in making others wrong.

7. Decide to see the value of infinite patience with yourself and others.

8. Learn to see value in living your life based on the belief that love is the answer to any problem you have now or any problem you think you have in the future.

9. Start to believe that when you stop complaining about your age, and about what may be happening to your body, your day will be more happy and peace-filled.

10. Be kind and tender to others as well as to yourself.

11. Be authentic, respectful and have the same interest in others as you do in yourself.

12. Choose to live in a consciousness of giving instead of just getting.

13. Listen to all others, with no exceptions, with unconditional love.

14. Let go of all of your judgments.

15. See the value of being infinitely

patient with yourself, others, and the circumstances of your life.

16. Remember that finding things to be grateful for each day is the key to having a happy life.

17. Choose to live your life in grace—and laugh a lot.

18. See the Light in everyone rather than their lampshade.

19. Imagine that there is a 4-year-old child inside your heart, who is playful, who lives in the present, who cannot tell time yet, who doesn't yet understand the difference between yesterday and tomorrow, who likes to be silly and laugh and giggle most of the time, for no particular reason.

20. Look beyond the body and see the innocence and Light in everyone including your self.

21. Choose to be a love-finder rather than a fault-finder.

22. Choose to believe the truth that there is no value in worrying about anything—that to worry is a decision to suffer.

23. No matter what is going on in your body, choose spiritually to be fully alive, and not half-dead, and to celebrate your spiritual core inside your heart.

24. Make decisions by following your heart rather than your head.

25. Decide to let the sun shine in your heart regardless of the weather outside.

26. When you get stuck in life or in your head, remember that music can set you free.

27. Make "Loving Kindness" your song of the day, every day.

28. Choose to have faith and trust in

something that is higher than yourself.

29. Choose to act every day and night as if compassion was the center of your DNA—which it really is!

30. Remember that only the strong can ever dare to be gentle.

31. By seeing the value of letting go of fear and experiencing love, you can find it safe to become transparent and translucent. And free!

32. When you choose to believe that life is eternal, death need not be viewed as fearful.

33. If you find you are having a bad day, re-focus your thoughts on helping someone else.

34. Another way of looking at health is to see it as inner peace and healing as the letting go of fear.

35. Choose to make a decision—and totally believe it—that this day is going to be the happiest day of your life, regardless of what is put on your plate, and regardless of the state of your body.

Chapter 6

How We Use Aging With Attitude

Jerry is in his ninth decade of life and Diane is in her seventh at the time of this writing. We do not look at age as a number. Rather, we each choose to think of our self-identity as Spirit, which is ageless.

We continue to look upon ourselves as "works in progress," striving to be in a Higher Consciousness by doing our best to incorporate and live the Principles of

Attitudinal Healing and the Guidelines of Aging with Attitude.

We strive to make forgiveness and letting go of our judgments, guilt, and anger as parts of our daily practice. We do our best to watch what we put in our mouths and what we put into our minds.

We practice meditation daily. And we go to the gym five to six times a week for an hour and a half each time. We also start the day with gratitude and seeing Inner Peace as our only goal.

We remain passionate and happy beyond our previous expectations, feeling useful, focusing our lives of service on bringing Attitudinal Healing to people who have requested it around the world. This, by the way, does not feel like work but pure joy.

We find that all of the above works quite well for us, if not always perfectly. And we are happy to say that we no longer have any fears or worries about aging.

One of the most important practices that we have created to heal our own attitudes about aging is the daily way we greet the morning, shared in the following chapter.

Chapter 7

A Way of Starting the Day

We have often been asked about our personal spiritual practice and how we start the day. We do not intend this to be a model for others—we just want to share what works for us. We feel it is essential to start our day with a spiritual foundation. It renews us each day by beginning with a gentle way to greet the morning.

When we remind ourselves how we want to proceed through the day, we remember Love is our only reality instead of giving focus to our fears. This is a way of reminding us that in the real world, there is no past or future; there is only the eternal now.

We usually set our alarm clock for 4:00 a.m. We frequently receive phone calls from all over the world at various times of day. Therefore, we enjoy the still and quiet of the early morning hours, and use this time to devote attention to our spiritual core. We are not suggesting that anyone else should awaken this early, just noting that it works very well for us.

Upon awakening, we lie next to each other on our backs and hold hands as we invite each other to greet the morning. In silence, we each give gratitude for another day of living and for all the gifts and lessons of the day ahead. Then we imagine Light streaming from that which connects us all, entering the top of our heads and slowly moving down through our entire bodies. Each part of us changes from matter to Light. We lie there as beings of Light, reminding ourselves that the Light of Love is our true identity.

We continue to lie in silence, remembering ourselves as Beings of the Light. Together we send our Light to people that we know may be going through challenging times, whether with an illness or a relationship problem or perhaps some other challenging circumstance. Then we recite aloud a modified poem from *A Course in Miracles* which goes like this:

- I am not a body, I am free, for I am still as Creation created me.
- Today I want Peace.
- The Peace of Creation is everything that I want.

- It is the aim of all my living here, the end that I seek.

- It is my purpose, my function and my life while I abide where I am not at Home.

Then together we share the following affirmations out loud:

- Our thoughts create our reality.

- We commit to making this day the happiest day of our lives regardless of what is put on our plate and regardless of the state of our bodies.

- Today we will have no thoughts, attitudes or actions that are hurtful to others or ourselves.

- It is only my own thoughts and attitudes that hurt me.

- Forgiveness toward ourselves and others is the key to happiness.

- I am not a victim of the world I see.

- I commit to having inner peace as my only goal regardless of what is happening to me from the outside world.

- Your Light is all that I see, and it is but a reflection of the Light within me.

Perhaps because we wake up with a lot of energy in the morning, we always seem to have long to-do lists each day. And at the end of the day, with our lists still full of tasks, the temptation to feel guilty seems to hover above us. So one morning in meditation we were guided to create a To Be List, to celebrate our Spiritual Being as our true spiritual identity, rather than applauding our ego self which emphasizes form, physical bodies, fear, judgments, and guilt, and is constantly measuring ourselves against others.

Each morning we say the To Be List out loud to remind us to hold ourselves and all others, without exception, as our highest possible aspiration.

- I am Light of the World and so is everyone else.
- Today, my Spiritual Being is:

  Innocence

  Guiltless

  Judgeless

  Interpretless

  One That Is All With Life

  Spirit, Not a Body

  The Will of Creation

  Formless

  Limitless

  Timeless

  Ageless

  Fearless

  Angerless

  Eternal

  Happiness

Joyful

Unconditionally Loving

Unconditionally Forgiving

Blameless

Tenderness

Kindness

Patience

Compassion

Honesty and Integrity

Faithful

Trusting and Trustworthy

Gentle, Giving, Grateful and Generous

Open-Hearted and Open-Minded

Trusting and Trustworthy

Loving, Lovable and Loved

Translucent and Transparent

Unlimited and Unmeasureable

- I am the Universe's abundance that allows all resources to flow through me into the world without any boundaries, borders, or blocks, in total service and love.

We end our To Be List in gratitude for all the blessings and lessons in our lives.

Forgiveness Exercise

Forgiveness is important for our healing, so each morning we do a forgiveness exercise in our minds. It has become a powerful tool by which we break any negative energy and release all negative thoughts or grievances we might be holding against ourselves and others. Here is how we do the exercise:

Picture the face of someone you have a negative feeling towards or a grievance against. It could be someone from the past or from the present. They could be living or dead. They could be someone you know, or someone from the public you have never met (like a politician).

Imagine the person's face as very neutral in expression, close to your face. Behind this person, there is a bright, golden Light. This Light gets brighter while the person's face gets smaller and smaller as we say the following:

I forgive you…and I forgive myself

I thank you… and I thank myself

I love you… and I love myself

And I release you…and I release myself

And the person's face disappears into a tiny point of Light.

We then go deeper into the consciousness of sending our Light to those we know are suffering from disease, fear, and feeling a lack of love.

Next, we get out of bed, shower, get dressed, and light a candle that sits on a bronze statue of both our pairs of hands in prayer mode. One of us then reads out loud an inspirational lesson for the day.

Afterwards we meditate for twenty minutes, and then we spend a few moments discussing our experiences of the lesson and the meditation.

We then go to the gym where we exercise for about ninety minutes, after which we come home and have breakfast.

During the day, if we lose our feeling of peace over something, we have a phrase we use to get centered and back on track. One of us says to the other, "Are you willing to start the day over again?" The other agrees and with that agreement we mentally hit a reset button in our minds. This brings us back to the peace we felt after we had greeted the day. It really works! On particularly hectic days, we have been known to reset the button two or three times!

We find our morning's spiritual foundation is a
gentle way to greet the day, helping us remember
that we can choose to make all our decisions
based on love instead of fear, to remember that
we truly deserve the right to be happy, and to
teach only Love for that is what we are.

Chapter 8

REFLECTIONS ON LIFE FROM MY 9th DECADE

I have been blessed by many spiritual lessons in my 90-plus years. Today as I write these words, the following lessons and reminders have come to my mind, which I share with you here:

- Don't take my self so seriously.

- Laugh more easily and more whole-heartedly than ever before.

- Believe that nothing matters more than love and forgiveness.

- Love Nature more than ever before.

- At 60 I no longer cared what people said about me. At 91, it's even better because I can no longer remember what they have said about me.

- Unlearning is just as valuable to me as learning.

- Diane's Mom, Phyllis, was so correct when she taught me that when you are in your 90s you can get away with almost anything!

- I no longer feel embarrassed if someone points out that my zipper is down.

- I continue to surround myself with music I love and swing-dance my heart out with Diane whenever we can.

- I continue to become more consistent in no longer finding value in anger,

remembering more often that my attitude
is everything.

- Be gentle with myself and others.

- Let go more consistently of any guilt,
  blame, and shame.

- I remind myself daily that it is only my own
  thoughts and attitudes that can hurt me.

- The biggest gift the universe has given me
  is the power to choose the thoughts I put
  into my mind.

- Rejoice that I am no longer fearful
  of death.

- I am happier when I believe that all
  form is but an illusion and Love is
  letting go of form.

- I am not a victim of my blindness.

- Experience that my spiritual vision is
  getting better each day.

- See no value in worrying.

- Follow my heart rather than my head.

- Make all of my decisions, without exception, based on love instead of fear.

- Listen to the voice of Love within my heart to tell me what to think, what to say and what to do.

- Remember that I and everyone else are the Light of the World and that we are here to reflect it to each other.

- I delight in wearing my glasses that have LOVE printed across the lenses to remind myself and others to look at each other through the eyes of love.

- Practice going through a day and having no thoughts or actions that are hurtful to others or myself.

- See everyone else as my Siamese twin—as I love or hurt him, I love or hurt myself.

- Focus on giving rather than getting as the best way to live my life.

- Remember more often that love is always more powerful than fear.

- See no value in negative thinking.

- I am grateful beyond words that I stopped drinking in 1975, knowing that if I had not, I would no longer be here today.

- Know now that it is just as important to be kind to myself as it is to be kind to others.

- Know how important it is, regardless of my age, to exercise even a little each day.

- Believe that I was born with a spiritual DNA of happiness.

Recently, I spent seven weeks at the Western Blind Center for Veteran's to learn how to better navigate the world since I have become legally blind, with only extremely limited vision.

One day as I stepped out of my room and saw a whole group of veterans walking my way— all with their white canes. Three more vets with canes passed my room.

For a few moments I just stood there and experienced such great compassion for these men. Then I suddenly said to myself, "Jerry, you're blind and you walk with a white cane, too! You are one of them." In that moment, I learned that I need to be compassionate not only to others but to myself.

- Refrain from giving unsolicited advice as it is most often perceived as an attack.

- Remember that ultimately I do not know what is best for another person.

- Discover, as David Illili Kapralik said: "It is never too late to have a happy childhood."

- Commit to make this day the happiest day of my life, regardless of what is put on my plate and regardless of the state of my body.

- Conclude for myself that it keeps me in the present to give my love now and not wait for the future. I no longer wait for someone's funeral to share a eulogy about how much their love has meant to me. Why wait until then when I can call or visit today and touch another person's heart in a most meaningful way?

- I no longer believe I can be compassionate and angry at the same time.

- When I was 16, I wanted to be like Charles Atlas. He was a body builder who had a course on developing a muscular body just like his. The ads for his book were in magazines showing his big biceps and beautiful women feeling his muscles. I wanted to be like him and attract pretty women, too. At 91, I don't want to make my body attractive to women, but I do my best to keep my body in shape so that I can be healthy and be a better vehicle for love and peace.

- Today when I am stuck in my head, I remember that music can make me free.

- Today I do not believe in the concept of enemy—so I don't have any!

- In the early part of my life, I was very focused on my fear of dying. Today I am no longer afraid to leave my body. I know that I am spirit and I am free.

- I now focus on knowing that the purpose of relationships is joining, and the purpose of my fearful ego is separation.

- I used to think it was more important to talk with judgment and to listen with fearful, critical ears. I now feel that it is more important to just listen with love.

- My new definition for insanity is that we are insane when we are not experiencing ourselves as love and giving that love away. Which means that most of us are insane most of the time!

- I believe that surrendering to Love requires me to let go of the belief that my physical senses determine what is real.

- When I speak of my chronological age, my wife says that I am priceless. So I tell people that I am a walking antique.

Chapter 9

EVERY STEP OF THE WAY

To Age with Attitude

is to age with grace

and be positive about life.

It is to no longer see any value in

hurting another person or yourself

with words or with actions.

AGING WITH ATTITUDE

It is to consider that death

is but an illusion and a doorway

to Higher Consciousness.

Aging with Attitude

is to be free of fear

and making others wrong.

Aging with Attitude

is another way

of looking at the world;

It is to make forgiveness

as important as

breathing, and to love

all others as you would love yourself.

Aging with Attitude celebrates love every step of the way by living in the present and choosing to be happy, peaceful, guiltless, judgeless, and to be able to laugh at yourself and the world you see.

Epilogue

THE 12 PRINCIPLES OF ATTITUDINAL HEALING

1. The essence of our being is love.

2. Health is inner peace, healing is letting go of fear.

3. Giving and receiving are the same.

4. We can let go of the past and of the future.

5. Now is the only time there is and each instant is for giving.

6. We can learn to love ourselves and others by forgiving rather than judging.

7. We can become love finders rather than fault-finders.

8. We can choose and direct ourselves to be peaceful inside regardless of what is happening outside.

9. We are students and teachers to each other.

10. We can focus on the whole of life rather than the fragments.

11. Since love is eternal, death need not be viewed as fearful.

12. We can always perceive ourselves and others as either extending love or fearful and giving a call of help for love.

ABOUT THE AUTHORS

Gerald Jampolsky, M.D. is a Child and
Adult Psychiatrist and a graduate of Stanford
University School of Medicine. In 1975,
he founded the first Center for Attitudinal
Healing, in Tiburon, California. Now there are
independent Centers for Attitudinal Healing
throughout the world on five continents in
dozens of countries, offering free services for
children, adolescents and adults.

Diane Cirincione, Ph.D. is the Founder and Executive Director of Attitudinal Healing International. She is also a therapist in private practice, a businesswoman, author, and international lecturer. She serves on the Board of Directors of the World Business Academy as well as The Unstoppable Foundation.

Drs. Jampolsky and Cirincione are members of the faculty of the University of Hawaii School of Medicine, Department of Complementary and Alternative Medicine. Together and independently they have authored several bestselling books. Over the last four decades they have been invited to work together in over 60 countries and are recipients of numerous international awards.

In 2005, Dr. Jampolsky also received the *Excellence in Medicine—Pride in the Profession Award*, from the American Medical Association, for his lifetime humanitarian service and for his contribution of Attitudinal Healing to the field of health.

In 2015 both Drs. Jampolsky and Cirincione were awarded the Ellis Island Medals of Honor for living lives dedicated to helping others and sharing their personal and professional gifts for the benefit of humanity.

For more information visit:
www.AHInternational.org
or
www.DianeCirincione.com

You may also write to:
Attitudinal Healing International
3001 Bridgeway, Suite K-368
Sausalito, California, U.S.A. 94965
Phone 877-244-3392

OTHER BOOKS
BY THE AUTHORS

- A Mini Course for Life
- Love is the Answer
- Change Your Mind, Change Your Life
- Wake-Up Calls
- Finding Our Way Home
- Simple Thoughts That Can Change Your Life
- Me First and The Gimme Gimmes

By Gerald Jampolsky, M.D.

- Love is Letting Go of Fear
- Teach Only Love
- Good-Bye to Guilt
- Forgiveness: The Greatest Healer of All
- Out of Darkness, Into the Light
- Shortcuts to God
- One Person Can Make a Difference
- The "Oh Shit" Factor: Waste Management for Our Minds

By Diane Cirincione, Ph.D.

- Sounds of the Morning Sun

WHAT IS ATTITUDINAL HEALING?

Attitudinal Healing (AH) is a cross-cultural method of healing that helps remove self-imposed blocks such as judgment, blame, shame, and self-condemnation that are in the way of experiencing lasting love, peace, and happiness. Attitudinal Healing is based on the belief that it is not people or experiences outside of ourselves that cause us to be upset. Rather, it is our thoughts, attitudes, and judgments about them that cause us distress.

In Attitudinal Healing health is defined as inner peace and healing, as the letting go of fear. These are guiding principles in this groundbreaking work in personal, collective, and global transformation.

The approach and philosophy is based on universal principles and forgiveness. People of all ages, beliefs, walks of life, and cultures, volunteer, support, and benefit from the practice of Attitudinal Healing.

HISTORY OF ATTITUDINAL HEALING

The first Center for Attitudinal Healing was founded in 1975 by Gerald Jampolsky M.D. Attitudinal Healing is a widely recognized, award-winning, replicable model for inner healing that has been used successfully for four decades, both locally and in over 60 countries on 6 continents.

Since its inception Attitudinal Healing has organically grown around the world leading

to the formation of Attitudinal Healing
International (AHI). Its mission is to support
all established, independent Centers and
emerging Centers in their growth and
innovative adaptations of Attitudinal Healing.

The Principles of Attitudinal Healing have
inspired extraordinary strength in millions
of ordinary people to heal their own hearts
and minds by choosing peace over conflict,
compassion over indifference, and love
over fear.

ATTITUDINAL HEALING INTERNATIONAL

The mission of Attitudinal Healing
International is to support all established,
independent centers and emerging centers
in their growth and in their innovative
adaptations of Attitudinal Healing.

Attitudinal Healing International works
towards a world where each of us takes
responsibility for what we think, say, and do,

and where we each feel safe, whole and loved. Attitudinal Healing gives us the powerful tools needed for making healthy choices, navigating successful challenges, and creating positive change. This is accomplished by our utilizing the Principles of Attitudinal Healing, enabling us to choose peace over conflict, compassion over indifference, and love over fear in all aspects of our daily lives.

Visit www.AHInternational.org to learn about and connect with this growing worldwide community. The website includes information on the many centers and groups in over thirty countries around the world as well as on both online and on-site trainings. Learn about Attitudinal Healing Global Innovations and programs that make a difference in the world in the areas of health, education, addictions, institutions, business, and community.

ATTITUDINAL HEALING VIDEOS

View a wide selection of excellent videos on Attitudinal Healing at:

www.youtube.com/user/AHInternational

Don't miss this one:

Aging With Attitude Jerry Jampolsky
Jerry at 90 working out at the gym.
Great musical background, with thoughtful, inspirational quotes on aging.

And check out:

Forgiveness: An Interview with Jerry Jampolsky and Diane Cirincione
Georgia Shakti-Hill's interview on the show *Living in Balance*.

Made in the USA
San Bernardino, CA
05 December 2017